GW00660043

Cover illustration: *Teniente de Navío* Luis Antonio Collavino poses next to Super Etendard 3-A-204 at Comandante Espora Naval Air Station; note the French Navy issue flying gear. Collavino was wingman to *Capitán de Corbeta* Alejandro Francisco during the 30 May mission against the British Task Force, in which the Argentines claimed to have damaged HMS *Invincible*.

1. This photograph, taken late in April 1982, shows Mirage IIIEA I-016 taxiing to the runway at Dr. Mariano Moreno air base en route to Comodoro Rivadavia. This aircraft flew seven air cover sorties during the war. On 8 October 1983 it was badly damaged (but reparable) at Rio Gallegos, when its pilot, *Capitán* González – one of *Grupo* 8's most experienced officers – attempted a slow roll on finals with the wheels down and carrying two 1,700-litre drop tanks and a pair of Matra R.550 AAMs. The aircraft landed beside the runway, tearing away its landing gear and much of the belly. For this, *Capitán* González was grounded for over a year!

WARBIRDS ILLUSTRATED NO. 45

ARGENTINE AIR FORCES
in the Falklands Conflict

SALVADOR MAFÉ HUERTAS &
JESÚS ROMERO BRIASCO

ARMS AND ARMOUR PRESS

First published in Great Britain in 1987 by Arms and Armour Press Ltd., Link House, West Street, Poole, Dorset BH15 1LL.

Distributed in the USA by Sterling Publishing Co. Inc., 2 Park Avenue, New York, NY 10016.

Distributed in Australia by Capricorn Link (Australia) Pty. Ltd., P.O. Box 665, Lane Cove, New South Wales 2066.

British Library Cataloguing in Publication data:
Huertas, Salvador Mafé
Argentine Air Force in the Falklands Conflict.—
(Warbirds illustrated; 45).
1. Argentina—Fuerza Aérea   2. Falkland Islands War, 1982
I. Title   II. Briasco, Jesús Romero   III. Series
997′.11   F3031.5

ISBN 0-85368-819-2

Edited and designed by Roger Chesneau; typeset by Typesetters (Birmingham) Ltd., printed and bound in Great Britain by The Bath Press, Avon.

◀ 2
2. After successfully attacking the frigate *Ardent* on 21 May, *Capitán de Corbeta* Alberto Jorge Philippi was shot down over the Falklands Sound by a Sea Harrier flown by Lt. Morrell of 800 NAS. Having survived in the desolate west coastal region of East Falkland for several days, he was picked up by some kelpers who treated him very well and handed him over to the Argentines, and he returned to Río Grande on 29 May. The Skyhawk carries the *3ª Escuadrilla* insignia beneath the cockpit.

Introduction

This book is a pictorial account of the role played by Argentina's air forces during the short but bitter struggle with Great Britain for the possession of the inhospitable Falkland Islands in the spring of 1982. Argentina deployed about 300 aircraft of all types in the islands and from southern mainland air bases, losing 100 to all causes. In combat, two aircraft emerged with a high reputation. The record of the Dassault Super Etendard, from the *Comando de Aviación Naval*'s *2ª Escuadrilla de Caza y Ataque*, speaks for itself. Working up to operational efficiency without French assistance, four aircraft and five Exocet missiles destroyed two British ships and to a large degree conditioned the activities of the Task Force, especially those of the carriers. Second, the *Fuerza Aérea*'s elderly A-4B Skyhawks from *Grupo 5 de Caza*, using only free-fall bombs, destroyed three British ships and damaged many more in the course of 133 combat sorties, albeit losing ten aircraft and nine pilots.

In terms of tactics, Argentine aviators were lacking somewhat compared to the standards practised by their British counterparts, and some of their losses could doubtless have been avoided had there been some kind of mutual support. The 1 May air battle, in which two Mirage IIIEA interceptors were lost to a pair of Sea Harriers, clearly showed their inability to wrest air superiority from the very effective V/STOL interceptors, a problem aggravated by the aircraft's lack of range. In a sense, however, what was lacking in tactics was in large measure made good by courage and determination. Transport and helicopter pilots also deserve mention, especially the C-130 Hercules crews, who made many daring resupply flights to Port Stanley as well as carrying out some highly dangerous surveillance sorties. Most of the aircrews from the three services got notice of the landings during the early hours of 2 April. They were ill-prepared for the kind of conflict that ensued, having directed their training towards possible hostilities with Chile arising out of the long-standing dispute over the sovereignty of the Beagle Channel.

From 2 April to 14 June 1982 the *Fuerza Aérea Argentina* recorded 12,454 flight-hours, of which 2,782 were by combat jets. A total of 505 combat sorties were planned for fighter/attack aircraft based on the mainland, and of these 272 reached their targets; in addition, the Falklands-based IA-58 Pucarás made more than 100 combat sorties. FAA transport aircraft made 421 landings at Port Stanley in April and 31 between 1 May and 13 June. The *Comando de Aviación Naval* flew a total of 550 sorties from 2 April to 14 June involving all types of missions from the mainland and the islands. Finally the Argentine Army's *Batallón de Aviación de Combate 601* helicopters deployed to the Falklands recorded 796 missions, with 1,011 flight-hours.

The photographs presented here have come from a variety of sources in Great Britain and Argentina. Many originate in private collections on both sides of the Atlantic and are manifestly not the work of professional photographers, but their historic interest is considerable, capturing as they do the atmosphere of the war and recording the Argentine air forces' baptism of fire and the high price which was paid.

Salvador Mafé Huertas
Jesús Romero Briasco

▲ 3

▲ 4   ▼ 5

3. At the time of the Falklands War the *Fuerza Aérea Argentina* possessed three Boeing 707s, assigned to the El Palomar (Buenos Aires) based *I Brigada Aérea, Grupo 1 de Transporte, Escuadrón II*. Their main task was the long-range transport of personnel and freight, and although they could not operate from Port Stanley's short runway they maintained a 'shuttle service' flying men and equipment to the southern mainland air bases – an unglamorous but vital role in support of the combat units.

4. The Boeing 707s were also pressed by the FAA's high command into other more warlike roles, such as reconnaissance and surveillance. On 21 April 1982, aircraft TC-91 carried out the first such sorties in search of the British Task Force, which it detected at about 0900hrs, soon after the Argentine aircraft was intercepted high over the South Atlantic by an 800 NAS Sea Harrier flown by Lt. Simon Hargreaves. Another, more risky incident for the 707 aircrews occurred on 22 May, when an *Escuadrón II* aircraft took violent action to avoid four Sea Dart missiles launched by two Royal Navy destroyers.

5. Both the *Fuerza Aérea Argentina* (in the form of *I Brigada Aérea, Grupo I de Transporte, Escuadrón II*) and the *Comando de Aviación Naval* (*2ª Escuadrilla Aeronaval de Apoyo Logístico*) operated the Fokker F.28 Fellowship twin-jet transport, flying numerous supply runs in the so-called 'air bridge' between mainland bases and Port Stanley airfield during the fighting. The FAA aircraft operated from *Base Aérea Militar* Comodoro Rivadavia and the *Aviación Naval* F.28s from the *Base Aeronaval* Río Grande. Seen here at Comodoro Rivadavia in May 1982, F.28 TC-51 is readied for a supply flight to Port Stanley.

6. The ubiquitous Fokker F.27 Friendship was operated by *I Brigada Aérea, Grupo I de Transporte, Escuadrón IV*, also being loaned to the LADE airline as and when needed. During the war most of the operational aircraft were based at Comodoro Rivadavia, whence a few supply flights were flown to Port Stanley, but the majority of the sorties undertaken by these transports were for surveillance or search and rescue, or to act as radio relay links for fighter-bomber missions. Illustrated is F.27 TC-76 at El Palomar air base, shortly before departing for Comodoro Rivadavia, April 1982.

7. At the beginning of the war the FAA had two C-130Es, five C-130Hs and two KC-130Hs on strength; this fleet was based at El Palomar, where it was one of the components of *I Brigada Aérea*, equipping *Escuadrón I* of *Grupo I de Transporte*. The Hercules was truly the FAA's workhorse during the conflict, and the mainstay of the air bridge. This interesting photograph, taken shortly before the crisis flared up, shows C-130H TC-68 after landing at Stanley en route to Vicecomodoro Marambio in Antarctica.

▲8

8. The two KC-130Hs were worked very hard during the war. Normally operating from BAM Río Gallegos, they flew 29 missions, refuelling 29 FAA Skyhawk flights, as well as twenty *Aviación Naval* A-4Q and Super Etendard sorties, and several of the Argentine air forces' successes in anti-shipping operations resulted only because of the assistance of the *chanchas* (mother sows), as the aircraft were known among their crews. This is TC-70 at Río Gallegos, May 1982.

9. FAA C-130s were quite a common sight at Port Stanley before the war. They were sometimes operated on behalf of the LADE airline, as in this photograph of a Hercules landing in the Falklands.

10. A C-130H (TC-66) at BAM Marambio, Argentine Antarctica,

framed by the tail of a *IX Brigada Aérea* DHC-6 Twin Otter light transport; shortly after this photograph was taken the small Hercules fleet was heavily committed in *Operación 'Azul'*, the occupation of the Falkland Islands by the Argentine forces. The Hercules aircraft carried out some daring long-range ocean surveillance missions, and in the course of such a sortie one of their number was shot down by a Sea Harrier on 1 June 1982.

11. A rare photograph taken shortly before the war showing a *Grupo 1* Hercules formation. C-130E TC-63, in the foreground, was shot down on 1 June 1982 by Lt. Cdr. Ward from 801 Naval Air Squadron.

▼9

▲12

▲13　▼14

12. The FAA's only photo-reconnaissance capability comprised four Lear Jet 35As, equipping *Grupo I Aerofotografico, II Brigada Aérea*. During the war the small fleet, based at Comodoro Rivadavia, was augmented by two FAA calibration Lear Jets as well as some impressed, ex-civilian machines and it conducted several high altitude sorties over the Falklands Sound and San Carlos Water. Illustrated is T-21 at Comodoro Rivadavia, May 1982.

13. In April 1982 the FAA possessed ten Canberra bombers, eight B.62s and two T.62s, forming *Grupo 2 de Bombardeo* of *II Brigada Aérea* based at Parana in the province of Entre Rios. Shortly after the Falklands invasion eight aircraft were deployed to *Base Aeronaval* Trelew, Chubut Province, and from there the ageing bombers operated during the entire war, although some sorties were flown from Río Gallegos and Río Grande. From this latter airfield *Grupo 2* made the first FAA combat sortie of the war, when on 26 April 1982 three Canberras took off from Río Grande to attack British shipping near South Georgia.

14. *Grupo 2* Canberras planned 54 bombing sorties during the fighting; 46 were flown, of which 25 were completed successfully.

Two aircraft were lost. B-110 was shot down on 1 May 160nm north of Port Stanley by an 801 NAS Sea Harrier; the crew, comprising *Teniente* de Ibañez and *Primer Teniente* Gonzalez, ejected but neither man was ever found. This photograph shows a T.64 and two B.62s at Trelew.

15. The IA-58A Pucará, an Argentine-designed and built counter-insurgency (COIN) aircraft, was the only FAA combat aeroplane to be based on the Falklands Islands during the war. The first four Pucarás were flown from Río Gallegos to Port Stanley on 2 April 1982, shortly after the occupation was completed and as soon as the airfield's runway had been cleared of obstacles. Eventually a total of 24 machines would be deployed to the islands; none returned to the mainland. Illustrated here shortly before the war, Pucará A-518 was deployed to Santa Cruz airfield.

16. Of the twenty-four Pucarás lost on the Falklands, only four were destroyed in the air. Besides A-537, these were A-511, by a Sea Harrier on 21 May; A-531, on the same day, by a Stinger missile; and A-555, on 28 May, by a combination of Blowpipe missile and small-arms fire.

17. An IA-58A Pucará from *Grupo 3 de Ataque* photographed at Comodoro Rivadavia, May 1982. Note the theatre identification markings and the 19-round 2.75in rocket pods. The fixed armament comprises four 7.62mm machine guns and two 20mm cannon.

18. A-522 in a light camouflage scheme seen at Río Gallegos before departing for the Falkland Islands, May 1982. As well as rocket pods the aircraft carries three napalm canisters on the centreline weapons station. This Pucará was located by British forces at Stanley and was taken to the United Kingdom aboard *Contender Bezant*.

19. A pair of IA-58A Pucarás from *Grupo 3 de Ataque* overfly the '*Pampa*' during their deployment from Reconquista to Comodoro Rivadavia. The aircraft are in ferry configuration.

17 ▶

▼18

▲20

▲21   ▼22

20. Taken by the F95 camera of a Sea Harrier, this aerial photograph shows Pebble Island's airstrip (renamed by the Argentinians BAN Calderon) shortly after the devastating SAS raid, in which eleven aircraft were destroyed or immobilized. Note the Beech T-34C and the IA-58A Pucará only lightly damaged.

21. A view of A-512, taken at Santa Cruz, at which airfield a Pucará 'pool' was established to provide replacements for the islands-based squadron. Besides the aircraft lost during the fighting, another one, A-540 from *Grupo 4 de Ataque*, crashed into the sea on 24 May during a reconnaissance mission near Comodoro Rivadavia. The pilot, Alferez Valko, was killed.

22. Pucará A-515, seen at Stanley after the fighting had ceased; note the hastily applied camouflage over the natural metal finish. In the background can be seen the remains of the Falkland Islands Government Air Services Britten-Norman BN-2A-27 Islander VP-FAY, which had been impressed by the FAA and was destroyed on 1 May 1982 during the Sea Harrier raid.

23. A-515 was taken to Britain and, bearing the serial ZD485, was test-flown at A&AEE Boscombe Down, where its handling qualities were considered to be very good.

24. A Sea Harrier pilot poses in front of several wrecked Pucarás at Port Stanley after the Argentine surrender on 14 June 1982. Note the bomb damage to the starboard wing of the aircraft in the foreground.

25. In April 1982 the FAA had twelve North American F-86F Sabres available on the strength of *Escuadrón II* of *IV Brigada Aérea*, based at BAM Mendoza. These elderly aircraft were used as operational trainers for fighter-bombers pilots, but after the Argentine occupation of the Falklands Islands the FAA studied the possibility of basing a detachment at Stanley airfield. Tests were conducted at Mendoza, where the runway was painted to simulate the space available at Stanley, but the idea proved impractical. Here three Sabres are seen shortly before their departure to Comodoro Rivadavia, June 1982.

23 ▲

24 ▲   25 ▼

▲ 26

▲ 27　▼ 28

26. Twenty-five reconditioned A-4C Skyhawks were delivered to the FAA in 1976 from US Navy surplus stocks, forming the *'Escuadrón Skyhawk'* of *Grupo 4 de Caza-Bombardeo* of *IV Brigada Aérea*, based at Mendoza. The aircraft differed from the A-4Bs in having two extra hardpoints and an updated nav/attack system of British origin. At the start of the conflict this unit had eighteen A-4Cs, most of which were deployed to San Julian airfield in Santa Cruz Province in mid April. The aircraft illustrated, C-302, flew five combat sorties during the war.

27. The *Grupo 4* A-4C Skyhawks were camouflaged in 'desert' colours, with brown and sand uppersurfaces with light grey undersurfaces. This unit lost nine aircraft during the fighting, thus having the dubious honour of being the FAA fighter-bomber *Grupo* with the highest percentage of aircraft losses, both in terms of original strength and of sorties flown. The photograph shows two A-4Cs taking off from Mendoza bound for San Julian, April 1982.

28. Besides being the unit with the most losses (nine aircraft and eight pilots), *Grupo 4 de Caza* was also the least successful, with confirmed credit only for damage to a few British ships, in spite of Argentinian claims to the contrary. This is C-318, which took part in several raids.

29. This interesting photograph shows an A-4C refuelling from a KC-130H en route to its target. Yellow theatre identification markings appear on the vertical fin, the wing root and the undersides of the drop tanks; note also the 500lb bomb (of British origin). This Skyhawk formed part of 'Jaguar' Flight, which left unexploded bombs on board *Sir Lancelot* and *Sir Galahad* in San Carlos Water on 24 May while losing one of their number.

30. Nose detail of the A-4C in which Alferez Isaac and three other *Grupo 4* pilots attacked British ships in San Carlos Water on 25 May 1982. Although the aircraft is painted up with the silhouette of a Type 22 frigate, in reality the mission failed, and cost two aircraft and one pilot. Note the *Grupo 4 de Caza* crest.

31. Nose detail of one of two A-4C survivors of the attack on the Task Force in 30 May 1982, in which the Argentinians claimed that they had damaged HMS *Invincible*; in fact they had attacked, unsuccessfully, the frigate *Avenger*. Note the Falkland Islands 'map' next to the unit crest.

29 ▲

30 ▲   31 ▼

▲ 32   ▼ 33

32. An air-to-air view of an A-4C taking on fuel from a KC-130H tanker. The Skyhawk carries a multiple ejector rack on the centreline, with four Israeli-made 500lb bombs. C-312 was crewed by Alferez Gerardo Isaac during an attack against British ships in San Carlos Water; it was damaged by anti-aircraft hits on its fuel system and was lucky to return to base.

33. Six A-4Cs on the flight line at Mendoza shortly after the war; note the F-86F Sabres in the background. During the war the aircraft detached to the south were dubbed '*Escuadrón A-4C San Julian*'. Planned combat missions numbered 106, of which 86 were flown and 41 resulted in the aircraft attacking their targets.

34. The FAA's crack combat unit was *Grupo 5 de Caza, V Brigada Aérea*, based at Villa Reynolds. Nicknamed '*Los Halcones*' ('The Hawks'), the *Grupo* was composed of two *escuadrónes* and by March had on strength about 36 A-4B Skyhawks (although not all serviceable) from a total of 50 refurbished machines received between 1966 and 1970. The photograph depicts C-240, which on 21 May 1982, crewed by *Teniente* Robledo, formed part of 'Orion' Flight, which damaged the frigate HMS *Argonaut*. Note the position of the *Grupo 5 de Caza* insignia, a hawk's head.

19

▲35

35. After the war a modest modernization programme saw the surviving A-4Cs receive some improvements to their weapons and ECM systems. Amongst these was the capability to carry air-to-air IR missiles for self-defence, the aircraft being wired for both the Matra Magic and the Rafael Shafrir. The photograph shows an A-4C carrying eighteen bombs of Argentine manufacture, together with captive (acquisition) Shafrirs under the outboard pylons.

36. Two *Grupo 5 de Caza* Skyhawks begin refuelling on the way home from a combat sortie; the KC-130Hs saved several of these aircraft from meeting a watery end. *Grupo 5* deployed its first A-4Bs to Río Gallegos on 14 April 1982, from which base they operated for most of the war, although for the last days the unit was redeployed to San Julian.

37. *Teniente* Bolzan in aircraft C-237 returns to his dispersal at Río Gallegos after the first air attacks on 1 May 1982. This pilot lost his life when his aircraft, C-204, was shot down over Choiseul Sound on 8 June 1982 by an 800 NAS Sea Harrier. The wreckage of the Skyhawk fell on Rain Cove, Island Creek.

38. The elderly A-4B was the FAA's most successful combat aircraft, the pilots, from *Grupo 5 de Caza* '*Halcones*', causing the loss of HMS *Antelope*, HMS *Coventry* and RFA *Sir Galahad*, sharing in the sinking of HMS *Ardent*, and damaging HMS *Glasgow*, HMS *Argonaut* and RFA *Sir Tristam* among others. Illustrated is C-225, which, flown by *Teniente* Barrionuevo, took part in the attack on *Coventry*.

▼36

▲39

39. *Grupo 5* armourers paint some messages on bombs to be fitted to an A-4B at Río Gallegos, May 1982.

40. *Grupo 5 de Caza* planned 133 sorties and carried out 86. In this photograph *Teniente* Luis Alberto Cervera ('Tucu') demonstrates the altitudes from which the A-4Bs typically made their attacks.

41. A-4B C-236 shortly after the war, inside a hangar at Villa Reynolds. Five ship silhouettes are painted in yellow on its side.

▲40 ▼41

42. Nose detail of A-4B C-207 at Río Gallegos. Again, note the ship silhouettes (one of which represents *Coventry*), and also the flight bag and 'bone dome' hanging from the barrel of the 20mm cannon.

43. The five ship 'kills' shown on A-4B Skyhawk C-236 probably reflect the total number of ships sunk and damaged by *Grupo 5 de Caza*. After the war all the surviving A-4Bs had Omega navigation systems installed; before the conflict only one-third of the fleet had this device.

42▲   43▼

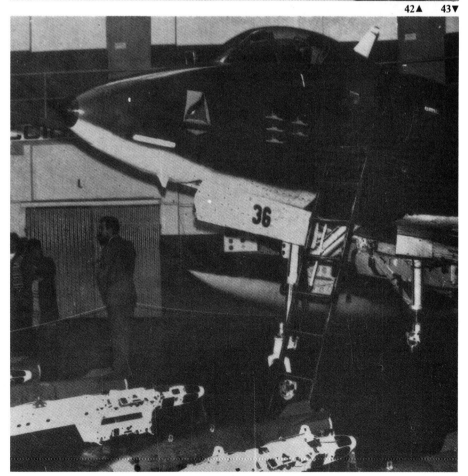

44. *Primer Teniente* Cervera (left) and *Primer Teniente* Sánchez pose in front of A-4B C-236 at Río Gallegos. The latter pilot was the only survivor of '*Mazo*' Flight, three out of the four Skyhawks of which were shot down on 8 June 1982 near Fitzroy by 800 NAS Sea Harriers.

45. Four *Grupo 5 de Caza* pilots pose beneath one of their A-4Bs. Second from the right is *Capitán* Carballo, one of the FAA's most successful attack pilots; to his left is *Teniente* Lucero (posted from *Grupo 4*), who on 25 May was shot down over San Carlos Water in A-4C C-319 and was taken prisoner. A British-made 1,000lb bomb hangs beneath the aircraft.

46. A flight of three *Grupo 3 de Ataque* Pucarás near Reconquista; the aircraft's rugged lines can be seen to advantage. A-514 and A-515 were assigned to the so-called '*Escuadrón Pucará Malvinas*' and were found by British forces at Stanley airfield. The former was heavily damaged by bomb blast, but the latter was taken to Britain for evaluation.

47. During the war *Grupo 5 de Caza* lost ten A-4B Skyhawks; nine of its pilots were killed and one ejected over West Falkland Island. Illustrated is A-4B C-207, in which *Primer Teniente* Velasco sank the Type 42 destroyer *Coventry* on 25 May.

▲ 44   ▼ 45

C-207

▲48   ▼49

48. The A-4Bs were camouflaged in dark green and brown, with light blue undersurfaces. Here A-4B C-226 is shown refuelling from a KC-130H Hercules; some time later, on 8 June, it would be shot down by an 800 NAS Sea Harrier near Choiseul Sound and its pilot, *Teniente* Juan José Arrarás, killed.

49. During the course of the war the *Grupo 6* Daggers were credited with 133 sorties, of which 81 were completed. The Daggers were camouflaged in a three-tone uppersurface scheme consisting of dark green, medium green and tan, while under surfaces were light grey. Here C-430 and C-419 are seen at San Julian on 24 May 1982; a couple of hours after the photograph was taken both had been shot down near Pebble Island by an 800 NAS Sea Harrier. Note the faded theatre markings, even on the drop tanks fitted to C-419.

50. The *Fuerza Aérea Argentina* received its first Mirage IIIEAs in June 1972, these comprising ten single-seat all-weather fighters and two dual-seat operational trainers; all entered service with the newly activated *VIII Brigada Aérea, Grupo 8 de Caza*, forming the '*Escuadrón Mirage III*'. In 1980 a second batch of seven Mirage IIIEAs was acquired, and shortly after the Falklands conflict ended a pair of refurbished ex-*Armée de l'Air* Mirage IIIBEs were also procured. Illustrated is I-006, at Comodoro Rivadavia with armourers in the process of loading the Defa 553 cannon.

51. Mirage 5P C-403 took its serial from a Dagger flown by *Capitán* Donadille which was destroyed by a Sea Harrier on 21 May. This aircraft was photographed inside a maintenance hangar at Dr. Mariano Moreno air base, home of *Grupo 8 de Caza*. The Mirage 5Ps are now receiving modifications and updates similar to those applied to the Daggers.

▲52

▲53 ▼54

55 ▲

52. Taken at Río Gallegos shortly after the war, this photograph shows two *Group 8 de Caza* Mirage IIIEAs being readied for a practice air-to-ground sortie.

53. Of the six MB.339As deployed by *1ª Escuadrilla de Ataque*, under the command of *Capitán* de Corbeta Molteni, five were lost: one was written off in an accident, another was shot down by a Blowpipe missile, and the remaining three were abandoned at Stanley airport to be captured by British forces.

54. The Beechcraft T-34C-1 Turbo Mentor is essentially a basic trainer but it can be converted into a light attack aircraft. The Argentine Navy acquired fifteen; deliveries were completed in 1980, and the Turbo Mentors entered service with the *Escuela de Aviación Naval*, the combat element of which is the *4ª Escuadrilla Aeronaval de Ataque* based at Punta del Indio. On 23 and 24 Apri 1982 six T-34Cs were deployed from Río Grande to Port Stanley and on 29 April from there to the little airstrip on Pebble Island. Seen here shortly after the conflict is a *4ª Escuadrilla* division in wartime camouflage.

55. The FAA received the first of 39 Daggers (Israeli-built Mirage 5s) in November 1978. Known in the Israeli Air Force as Neshers, the aircraft were built by IAI without licence. Between the above date and December 1980 a total of 26 refurbished machines had been received; later, between May 1981 and February 1982, a second batch of 13 machines was delivered. Of the total, four were dual-seat operational trainers.

56. *Teniente* Aguirre, a *Grupo 6 de Caza* pilot, who took part in an attack against three Royal Navy warships shelling Port Stanley airfield on 1 May 1982, *Glamorgan*, *Alacrity* and *Arrow*. The Dagger pilots claimed to have damaged two of the vessels, although the only one to suffer was *Arrow*, hit by nine 30mm rounds. In the photograph Aguirre is posing beside C-432, which was in fact the Dagger assigned to the leader of 'Torno' Flight during this attack; note the two-colour 'kill' marking, to indicate a damaged ship. San Julian, May 1982.

◀56

57. On 24 May 1982 *Grupo 6 de Caza* launched several Dagger sorties from San Julian and Río Grande. A flight of three was destroyed by Sea Harriers, but two other flights, '*Azul*' and '*Oro*', with a total of seven aircraft, reached San Carlos Water undisturbed, damaging with their bombs two British tank landing ships. The seven Daggers returned unscathed to Río Grande. The photograph shows the aircraft of '*Azul-3*' (*Capitán* Maffeis) low over *Sir Bedivere*.

58. Four *Grupo 6 de Caza* pilots – from left to right, *Capitán* Dimeglio, *Primer Teniente* Román, *Primer Teniente* Callejo and *Teniente* Aguirre Faget – pose in front of Dagger C-412. Note the 'kill' marking and the three 1,300-litre drop tanks. The photograph was taken at San Julian air base in May 1982.

59. Late in the war, as most Mirage IIIEAs from *Grupo 8 de Caza* were redeployed to Río Gallegos, a four-Dagger detachment was sent to Comodoro Rivadavia for air defence duties. Here *Primer Teniente* Callejo climbs into the cockpit of Dagger C-401 for a combat air patrol over the air base approaches. The aircraft is armed with two Shafrir IR-homing air-to-air missiles, one of which is just visible to the right of the ground crewman in the foreground.

◄ **57**

▲ 60

60. Spot the aircraft! Taken on 24 May, this spectacular photograph shows 'Oro-1' (*Capitán* Dellepiane) passing close to HMS *Fearless*.

61. Three Daggers at the alert ramp at San Julian, May 1982. Yellow identification markings are visible on fins and drop tanks.

▼ 61

62. Dagger C-421 during turn-around at San Julian. Ground crews experienced very difficult operating conditions at southern mainland air bases during the war.

62 ▲

63. Pilots from '*Escuadrón Dagger San Julian*' pose beside aircraft C-412, which has a 'kill' marking denoting a damaged ship. Note the mix of French and American 'bone domes'.

63 ▼

64. Detail showing damage caused by shrapnel from British anti-aircraft fire to the VHF antenna of a San Julian-based Dagger.
65. A *Grupo 6* armourer checks some Shafrir IR-guided air-to-air missiles. In the background is Dagger C-420.
66. *Capitán* Horacio Mir González poses in front of Dagger C-418 at Río Grande.

66 ▶

▲64   ▼ 65

▲ 67

▼ 68

67. Pilots from the '*Escuadrón Dagger Río Grande*' at a naval air station on Tierra del Fuego, June 1982.

68. A *Grupo 6 de Caza* ground crewman shows a 7.62mm hit on the starboard intake shock cone of an FAA Dagger.

69. A dramatic gun camera frame taken by *Capitán* Moreno's Dagger during the attack on the destroyer HMS *Antrim* on 21 May 1982. One 1,000lb bomb entered the ship but failed to explode.

70. A gun camera frame from the Dagger flown by *Primer Teniente* José Luis Gabari Zoco during the 8 June 1982 attack on the frigate HMS *Plymouth*. Note the shell splashes.

71. A closer view of *Plymouth*, this time taken from the gun camera of *Mayor* Martinez' Dagger on 8 June.

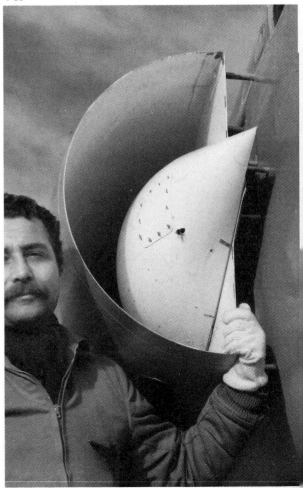

69 ▲   70 ▼   71 ▼

▲72

▼73

72. Shortly after the conflict most of the 26 surviving
Daggers were upgraded in a modernization
programme designed by Israel Aircraft Industries and
organized in three phases named, according to the
degree of sophistication, 'Finger Ia', 'IIa' and 'IIIa'.
The last phase provides the aircraft with a laser
rangefinder, an inertial navigation system, a head-up
display, ECM and an air-to-air refuelling capability.
Illustrated is C-415, with twelve Mk. 82 bombs and
two captive Shafrir AAMs.

73. Dagger C-401 took part in the attack against the
frigate HMS *Plymouth* on 8 June 1982, hence the
ship's silhouette applied to the nose. The pilot posing
here is *Primer Teniente* Cesar Roman, one of the
Grupo 6 de Caza officers with many combat missions
under his belt. The most unusual of these took place
on the day prior to the surrender, when as part of
'*Vulcano*' Flight he encountered HMS *Cardiff*'s Lynx
helicopter south of the Falklands. An old-fashioned
dogfight took place, but the helicopter pilot knew his
fighter evasion tactics well and avoided all the
Dagger's passes.

74. In June 1982 Peru supplied the FAA with ten
Mirage 5Ps as attrition replacements, these being
allocated to *Grupo 6 de Caza* and taking the serial
numbers of ten Daggers which had been lost during
the fighting. This Mirage 5P was photographed in
October 1982 at Río Gallegos, its serial, C-409, taken
from a Dagger flown by *Primer Teniente* Luna and
shot down by a Sea Harrier on 21 May that year. Note
the Peruvian 'desert' type camouflage scheme.

▲ 75

75. At the start of the war the FAA's helicopter force was concentrated in the *VII Brigada Aérea, Grupo 7 de Helicópteros*, which had its home base at BAM Morón, Buenos Aires, operating a mixed force of Hughes 369s, Aérospatiale SA.315B Lamas, UH-1Hs, Bell 212s, Sikorsky S-61Rs and CH-47C Chinooks. *Grupo 7* also impressed a number of civilian-owned helicopters, as shown by this Bell 212 on an SAR patrol out of Comodoro Rivadavia, June 1982.

76. Shortly after the invasion the FAA ordered a four-helicopter detachment, composed of two Bell 212s and both the Chinooks, to be stationed on the Falklands, and during the war this detachment flew 455 hours in the most adverse conditions, rescuing six Argentine pilots. Both 212s (H-83 and H-85) were abandoned, but the Chinooks flew back to the mainland on 9 June. Here Bell 212 H-86 tries some sling practice at Río Gallegos, May 1982.

77. This photograph, taken in March 1982, shows one of two S-61s from *Grupo 7*. On 2 April both were camouflaged and sent to Comodoro Rivadavia for long-range search and rescue work.

▲78　　　　　　　　　　　　　**▼79**

78. At the start of the war both CH-47Cs, deployed to
BAM Marmbio in Argentine Antarctica, were flown
back to Río Grande, where their grey and 'dayglo'
finish was replaced by a coat of camouflage paint,
internal fuel tanks were fitted and three machine guns
were installed for self-defence; by 11 April the
helicopters (H-91 and H-93) were operating in the
Falklands.

79. The peacetime operating base of *Grupo 8 de Caza*
is BAM Dr. Mariano Moreno, some 25 miles from
the city of Buenos Aires, but by late April 1982 ten
aircraft were deployed to BAM Comodoro Rivadavia
(headquarters of the Southern Air Force) and later to
Río Gallegos. In this photograph, taken in May 1982,
a *Grupo 8 de Caza* pilot climbs aboard Mirage IIIEA
I-004 for a local combat air patrol.

80. The Mirage IIIEAs in FAA service have a
camouflage scheme consisting of dark green, medium
green and tan uppersurfaces, with light grey
undersurfaces. Illustrated is I-007, at Dr. Mariano
Moreno shortly after the war and carrying a *VIII
Brigada Aérea* badge on the fin.

81. In the course of the shooting war *Grupo 8 de Caza*
Mirages planned 45 operational combat air patrol
sorties over the island, of which 39 were actually
carried out; two aircraft, I-015 and I-019, were lost,
both of them on 1 May during combat with Sea
Harriers. Here Mirage IIIEA I-005 is made ready at
Río Gallegos for an air cover sortie. Note the Matra
R.530 semi-active radar homing AAM on the
centreline and the 1,700-litre drop tanks.

▲ 82

▲ 83   ▼ 84

82. Only the second batch of Mirage IIIEAs had the capability to carry Matra R.550 Magic 'dogfight' missiles; in fact the first shipment of these AAMs had been received just a few weeks prior to the war and most *Grupo 8 de Caza* pilots were not fully trained with them. This Mirage IIIEA, I-017, is seen taking off from Río Gallegos for a patrol over the islands. It is equipped with two R.550s, one R.530 and two 1,700-litre drop tanks, and has its fin tip painted yellow.

83. Much has been written about the lack of success of *Grupo 8 de Caza* Mirages in contesting control of the air with the Fleet Air Arm's Sea Harrier force, but it must be borne in mind that the Mirage IIIEAs were operating at the limit of their combat radius – and then only at high altitude, in order to conserve fuel – and that the wily Sea Harrier pilots could not be enticed to fight at a tactical disadvantage. Here I-006 takes off for a high-level CAP. Note the Matra R.530; at least one of these missiles was fired against Sea Harriers on 1 May.

84. In fact the Matra R.530 was ill-suited to fighter-versus-fighter combat, and according to *Grupo 8* pilots its only purpose was to create a great deal of drag! This photograph shows I-014 departing for an operational mission. *Grupo 8* made the FAA's last combat sortie of the war when on the night of 13 June a Mirage IIIEA section flew escort for a pair of *Grupo 2* Canberras.

85. For only two short periods in the Falklands crisis were *3ª Escuadrilla* Skyhawks embarked aboard the carrier *25 de Mayo* – in late March/early April 1982 during *Operación 'Azul'*, and during late April/early May. A carrier battle almost took place on 2 May, when the six Skyhawks aboard *25 de Mayo* were loaded with bombs for attacking the British carriers, but light winds and the fact that the position of the British Task Force was 'lost' forced the cancellation. This photograph was taken during this tense period and shows 3-A-305 being prepared for its bomb load of suitably inscribed Snakeyes.

86. Towards the war's end some of the *3ª Escuadrilla Aeronaval de Caza y Ataque* Skyhawks received camouflage paint in order to make them less conspicuous over dark landscapes. Illustrated is 3-A-302, in a tan and green scheme.

▲87   ▼88

89 ▲

87. A Super Etendard is launched from *25 de Mayo*'s bow catapult. Another Super Etendard is parked on the starboard side, together with an A-4Q Skyhawk.

88. The A-4Qs' most successful sortie – and also its most unhappy experience – was on 21 May 1982, when three aircraft, led by *Capitán de Corbeta* Philippi, attacked and gave the *coup de grâce* to the damaged frigate HMS *Ardent* in Grantham Sound but were soon afterwards shot down by 800 NAS Sea Harriers. Two of the pilots survived, but another *3ª Escuadrilla* pilot was killed in a landing accident at Río Grande on 23 May, although the aircraft on this occasion sustained only light damage and was repaired.

89. A Grumman S-2E Tracker from *Escuadrilla Antisubmarina* is recovered aboard the carrier *25 de Mayo* after a reconnaissance sortie on 1 May 1982. The aircraft was looking for the British Task Force, but only radar emissions were detected.

90. On 2 April 1982 *1ª Escuadrilla de Helicopteros*, based at Comandante Espora, had nine Alouette IIIs and two Lynx HAS.23s on strength, most of them being embarked aboard ships of the Argentine Navy during *Operación 'Azul'*, the capture of the Falklands Islands and South Georgia. In the South Georgia operation an Alouette III embarked on the Antarctic supply ship *Bahía Paraiso* played a leading role in the success of the landings on 3 April 1982. During the war only one Alouette was lost, when the cruiser *General Belgrano* was sunk by the Royal Navy submarine *Conqueror* on 2 May.

90 ▼

▲ 91

91. Some of the Sea Kings had camouflage applied to make them less conspicuous, as illustrated by 2-H-233 seen here at Río Grande. Posing in front of the helicopter is *Capitán de Corbeta* Barro, the unit's CO, who, leading a two-aircraft formation, carried out a daring rescue mission from Río Grande to Pebble Island to recover Argentine personnel on 31 May 1982.

92. To replace some of its war losses, the FAA acquired nineteen Mirage IIICJs (C-701 to 719) and three Mirage IIIBJs (C-720 to 722) from surplus Israeli stocks. These arrived in Argentina between December 1982 and February 1983, to equip *Grupo 4 de Caza, IV Brigada Aérea*, at Mendoza and *Grupo 10 de Caza, X Brigada Aérea*, at Río Gallegos. Illustrated are a pair of the Mendoza-based Mirage IIICJs, modified to FAA standards.

▼ 92

93. This photograph, taken in June 1982, clearly shows the sort of operating conditions experienced at Río Gallegos during the war. A Mirage section is being readied for a combat sortie; in the background a *Grupo 5* A-4B Skyhawk is just discernible.
94. The Mirage IIIEA fleet was not employed in fighter-bomber duties because the aircraft were needed for air cover over the islands and for mainland interceptor duties; for most of the war the FAA believed that an attack by the Wideawake-based RAF Vulcans on mainland air bases or other military installations was a real possibility. Here I-017 is being manhandled out of a HAS at Río Gallegos.

▲ 95   ▼ 96

95. *Grupo 8 de Caza*'s only Mirage IIIDA dual-seater, seen here, flew some reconnaissance sorties from Comodoro Rivadavia during the conflict.
96. Mirage I-008, photographed at Dr. Mariano Moreno air base shortly after the war, flew three combat sorties from Río Gallegos.
97. The Mirage IIIEA flight line at Dr. Mariano Moreno shortly after the war.

98. Photographed here in October 1982 at Río Gallegos, these two Twin Otters belong to the Comodoro Rivadavia based *Grupo 9 de Transporte Aéreo, IX Brigada Aérea*, and aircraft T-83 still wears yellow identification stripes on the wings and tail. During the South Atlantic War these aircraft were used mainly on search and rescue duties.

98 ▼

▲99 ▼100

99. A close-up view of the nose of DHC-6 Twin Otter T-82, of *Grupo 9 de Transporte Aéreo*, which in a daring rescue operation to Pebble Island airlifted out a group of isolated FAA personnel to the mainland. The men included two Dagger pilots who had ejected and the body of a third.

100. An unusual formation comprising a *4ª Escuadrilla Aeronaval de Ataque* T-34C, a *2ª Escuadrilla Aeronaval de Caza y Ataque* A-4Q and a *1ª Escuadrilla Aeronaval de Ataque* MB.326GB.

101. Pictured here in prewar colours in March 1982 at Punta del Indio, this Macchi MB.339A was one of six from *1ª Escuadrilla Aeronaval de Ataque* deployed to Port Stanley. It crashed on approach to Port Stanley airfield on 3 May 1982, its pilot, *Teniente de Corbeta* Carlos Benitez, being killed.

102. T-34C-1 Turbo Mentor 0729/1-A-411 on display at the Fleet Air Arm Museum in Yeovilton. The notice on the starboard wing reads: 'This aircraft, used by the Argentinians during the occupation of the Falklands Islands in 1982, was disabled on the ground at Pebble Island on 15 May 1982 by units of 22 Special Air Service landed by naval helicopters of 846 Naval Air Squadron. It would not be available had it not been for the children of the Pebble Island Settlement who guarded and cared for it for over a year before making it available as a museum exhibit in the state you now see it.' Another three T-34Cs were destroyed or disabled during the SAS raid; the two surviving machines were flown back to Río Grande.

▲ 103

▲104 ▼105

103. Aircraft 4-A-115 was the only one of the six MB.339As deployed to the Falklands to return to the mainland; it is pictured here with a group of Navy support personnel. Note the gun and rocket pods, and also the wooden planks for parking the aircraft on soft ground to the side of the runway.

104. When found at Stanley after the Argentine surrender, this Macchi MB.339A was essentially intact although not airworthy. Note the theatre camouflage scheme and the yellow identification stripe around the rear fuselage.

105. Perhaps the only claim to fame of any of the *1ª Escuadrilla* MB.339As during the Falklands War was when *Teniente de Navío* Guillermo Owen Crippa made the first aerial sighting by the Argentines of the British landing force in San Carlos Water, counted twelve ships and single-handedly attacked the frigate *Argonaut*, slightly damaging her and escaping unscathed. This is 4-A-110 at the Fleet Air Arm Museum in Yeovilton, reassembled for exhibition using parts of 4-A-116.

106. During the period 1971–72 the *Comando de Aviación Naval* received sixteen refurbished A-4B Skyhawks from US Navy surplus stocks, which received the export designation A-4Q. These little attack aircraft equipped the *3ª Escuadrilla Aeronaval de Caza y Ataque*, based at Comandante Espora, Bahía Blanca, Buenos Aires, and the photograph shows eight of them in échelon formation shortly before the war. Aircraft 3-A-314 was shot down on 21 May by a Sea Harrier over the Falklands Sound, the pilot, *Teniente de Fragata* Marquez, being killed.

107. On 2 April 1982 *3ª Escuadrilla Aeronaval de Caza y Ataque* had ten A-4Qs available, and eight of these, together with twelve pilots, were deployed to Río Grande on 9 May 1982. A total of 45 sorties were planned during the war for these aircraft, but only on nine was the target reached. This is 3-A-305, aboard *25 de Mayo* in late March 1982.

▲108　▼109

110 ▲

108. The Argentine carrier *25 de Mayo* was commissioned into *Armada* service in March 1969. During the South Atlantic conflict she sortied twice, north of the Falklands, but did not see combat. In this photograph, taken shortly after the ceasefire, the ship is steaming in the South Atlantic with Skyhawks and Super Etendards on board.

109. The *2ª Escuadrilla Aeronaval de Caza y Ataque* was re-formed late in 1980 (it had previously been a T-28 Fennec unit), when a group of highly experienced A-4Q pilots and technicians were sent to France to train with the new Dassault Super Etendard, of which fourteen had been acquired. This photograph, taken shortly after the war, shows the *2ª Escuadrilla* flight line at Comandante Espora.

110. On 2 April 1982 *2ª Escuadrilla* had five Super Etendards on strength and a similar number of AM.39 Exocet missiles. The pilots carried out a rigorous training programme and by late April

deployed to Río Grande with four machines, the fifth (illustrated) being cannibalized to provide a source of spares following the French embargo on supplies.

111. The Super Etendard proved to be the most cost-effective combat aircraft operated by Argentina during the Falklands War, and its crews were undoubtedly the most professional: in ten combat missions, and with an expenditure of five Exocet missiles, they destroyed two British ships without loss to themselves. This unique photograph shows Super Etendard 3-A-202, flown by *Capitán de Corbeta* Francisco, refuelling from a KC-130H in company with FAA A-4Cs during the 30 May attack against the British Task Force. The Argentines claimed to have damaged HMS *Invincible* in this sortie but the boast proved to be a propaganda bluff.

111 ▼

▲ 112

▼ 113

112. *Capitán de Corbeta*
Augusto Cesar Bedacarratz in
the cockpit of a *2ª Escuadrilla
Aeronaval de Caza y Ataque*
Super Etendard. This pilot was
the leader of the section which
successfully attacked the Type
42 destroyer HMS *Sheffield* on 4
May 1982.

113. Río Grande, 1850hrs, 25
May 1982: *Capitán de Corbeta*
Roberto Curilovic climbs out of
his aircraft after a sortie which
lasted 4hr 7min in which
Atlantic Conveyor was hit by at
least one AM.39 Exocet.

114▲   115▼

114. *Teniente de Navío* Julio Héctor Barraza was Curilovic's wingman during the 25 May mission.

115. *Capitán de Corbeta* Curilovic (right) and *Teniente de Navío* Barraza beside Super Etendard 3-A-203, which was piloted by the senior officer during the 25 May mission. Note the 'kill' markings.

▲ 116

116. A close-up view of a *2ª Escuadrilla Aeronaval de Caza y Ataque* Super Etendard showing the *Sheffield* and *Atlantic Conveyor* silhouettes and the aircraft's unit markings.

117. Taken from the KC-130H tanker, this photograph shows aircraft 3-A-204, flown by *Teniente de Navío* Barraza, refuelling during the 25 May mission. Note the Exocet missile under the starboard wing.

▼ 117

118. A view of *25 de Mayo*'s flight deck on the afternoon of 1 May 1982. The windless conditions and the disposition of the British carriers *Hermes* and *Invincible* to the east prevented the *3ª Escuadrilla Aeronaval de Caza y Ataque* aircraft carrying out an attack with an adequate warload (i.e. six Mk.82 bombs).

119. This photograph, taken on 20 May 1982 at Río Grande, shows the full twelve-pilot complement of *3ª Escuadrilla Aeronaval de Caza y Ataque*. Standing, from left to right, are *Teniente de Fragata* Márquez (KIA), *Teniente de Navío* Lecour, *Teniente de Navío* Oliveira, *Capitán de Corbeta* Zubizarreta (killed in an operational accident), *Capitán de Corbeta* Philippi (shot down, ejected), *Capitán de Corbeta* Castro Fox (CO), *Teniente de Navío* Rotolo and *Teniente de Navío* Benitez; kneeling, left to right, are *Teniente de Fragata* Medici, *Teniente de Navío* Sylvester, *Teniente de Navío* Arca (shot down, ejected) and *Teniente de Navío* Olmedo.

▲ 120

120. A Grumman S-2E Tracker, 2-AS-23, from the *Escuadrilla Antisubmarina*, is launched from the carrier *25 de Mayo* on 1 May 1982 on a sortie to search for the British Task Force.

121. Only two Lockheed SP-2H Neptunes were available to the *Escuadrilla de Exploración* of the Argentine naval air arm. They were deployed from their usual base at Comandante Espora to Río Grande in Tierra del Fuego late in April, where surveillance missions were quickly scheduled. The Neptune's 'happy hour' took place on 4 May when aircraft 2-P-112 located and targeted HMS *Sheffield* for a *2ª Escuadrilla* Super Etendard section. The

photograph shows 2-P-111 shortly before being camouflaged in a low-visibility scheme, at Comandante Espora prior to deploying to Río Grande.

122. On the eve of the war the *Comando de Aviación Naval* had five Sikorsky S-61D-4 Sea Kings on strength for anti-submarine and troop transport duties, assigned to *2ª Escuadrilla de Helicopteros*. During hostilities they were also used in the casevac, surveillance and long-range search and rescue roles. The photograph shows 2-H-231 while operating from the Antarctic support vessel *Almirante Irizar* off Port Stanley, 2 April 1982.

▼ 121

123. On 2 April 1982 two *1ª Escuadrilla de Helicopteros* Lynx HAS.23s were embarked aboard the Argentine Navy Type 42 destroyers *Santisima Trinidad* and *Hercules*, supporting the landings in a variety of ways. Illustrated is 3-H-142, which on 2 May 1982 crashed in the sea not far from *Santisima Trinidad*.

124. The *Prefectura Naval Argentina* (Coast Guard) had a small aviation component, a detachment of which comprised two Short Skyvan light transports and an SA.330L Puma medium lift helicopter. Misfortune hit this little force: Skyvan PA-50 was destroyed by SAS commandos at Pebble Island on 15 May; Skyvan PA-54 was damaged early in the campaign by naval gunfire and destroyed shortly before the surrender by British artillery fire; and the Puma, PA-12, was damaged by naval gunfire on 4 May and was found in this state by British forces when they liberated Port Stanley. The helicopter was later taken back to Britain.

125. The crewmen from the *2ª Escuadrilla Aeronaval de Helicopteros* who on 31 May flew a daring rescue mission from Río Grande to Pebble Island: (left to right) *Suboficial* Montani, *Teniente de Navío* Brandeburgo, *Teniente de Navío* Oslvaldo Iglesias, *Capitán de Corbeta* Barro (CO), *Teniente de Navío* Guillermo Iglesias and *Suboficial* Giqueaux. In the background are the two SH-3s which took part in the mission, 2-H-233 being painted in brown and tan camouflage.

▲126

▲127   ▼128

126. In 1982 all the Argentine Army's helicopter assets were grouped within the *Batallón de Aviación de Combate 601* based at Campo de Mayo, Buenos Aires. During the period 9–29 April, nineteen helicopters were deployed to the Falklands by various means, three by direct flight, eight by sea and eight as air cargo. All were lost during the fighting, most being abandoned in various states of damage. Another Puma was destroyed by British small-arms fire during the landings at Grytviken on 3 April, while on 30 April another helicopter of the same type was destroyed inside the hangar on board the ice-breaker *Almirante Irizar* during a storm. Illustrated is an SA.330L, waiting to take on troops near Port Stanley.

127. The Pumas formed the 'Twin-Engine Helicopter Assault Company'. The wreck of the Puma shown in this photograph, AE-503, was part of a formation of three Pumas and an A.109 Hirundo which was caught by a pair of 800 NAS Sea Harriers near Shag Cove, West Falkland, on 23 May; three aircraft were destroyed, although none of the crews suffered casualties.

128. The wreckage of a UH-1H from the 'Single-Engine Helicopter Assault Company', seen after the Argentine surrender on Port Stanley racecourse. Note the yellow identification stripe.

129. UH-1H AE-422 was found by British forces at Port Stanley racecourse and was pressed into service by 820 and 825 NAS. It was later taken to the UK, ending its days on exhibition at the Fleet Air Arm Museum. Note the *B.Av.Com.601* insignia applied on the cockpit door.

130. The colour scheme applied to *B.Av.Comb.601* helicopters was overall olive drab, although some machines had yellow recognition markings. The three speedy A.109s deployed to the islands were under the command of the 'Attack Helicopter Company'; one, AE-337, was destroyed by Sea Harriers on 23 May, while the other two, AE-331 and 334, were found airworthy by British forces on Port Stanley racecourse and were taken back to the UK, where AE-334 was briefly exhibited at Yeovilton. After an overhaul both helicopters were taken into service by the Army Air Corps. Note the gun and rocket pods.

129▲ 130▼

▲131

▲132   ▼133

134▲

131. The final photographs in this book illustrate the major successes achieved by the Argentine air forces during the course of the Falklands War. On 4 May 1982, while on picket duty 70 miles south-west of Port Stanley, the Type 42 destroyer HMS *Sheffield* was hit by an Exocet missile launched by a *2ª Escuadrilla* Super Étendard. Twenty-one sailors died as a result of the attack, and the vessel sank six days later while under tow.

132. On 21 May 1982, while on fire support duties south of San Carlos Water, the Type 21 frigate *Ardent* was hit by bombs dropped by a *Grupo 6* flight and later by two flights of *3ª Escuadrilla* A-4Qs.

133, 134. San Carlos Water was nicknamed 'bomb alley' by British servicemen, and these photographs show dramatically how apt this was as vessels of the amphibious group are near-missed by Argentine bombs.

135. On 23 May 1982 the Type 21 frigate HMS *Antelope* was attacked in San Carlos Water by *Grupo 5* A-4B Skyhawks. One Skyhawk hit the ship's mainmast, but the bombs did not explode, although later that evening one did so while it was being defused.

135▼

136. A great fire engulfed the unfortunate *Antelope*, which blew up and sank. Early the next day only the bows and stern were visible, marked by a pall of white smoke.

137. On 25 May, while 90 miles north-east of Port Stanley and heading to San Carlos Water, *Atlantic Conveyor* was hit by one of two Exocets launched by a pair of *2ª Escuadrilla* Super Etendards. Following the missile's explosion upon impact, fire engulfed the vessel, destroying ten helicopters and large quantities of supplies and killing twelve crew members.

138. The Type 42 destroyer HMS *Coventry* was sunk by *Primer Teniente* Velasco from *Grupo 5 de Caza* with three 1,000lb bombs on 25 May 1982 some 10 miles north of Pebble Island.

139. The amphibious ship *Sir Galahad* was attacked by *Grupo 5* Skyhawks on 8 June while landing British troops at Fitzroy. The ship was severely damaged and was scuttled as a war grave on 26 June.

▲137

▲138   ▼139